Mike and Chip

by **Carl M. Polaski**
illustrations by **Sam Day**

Harcourt Brace & Company

Orlando Atlanta Austin Boston San Francisco Chicago Dallas New York Toronto London

"Chip," said Mitch.

"Let's play fetch!"

"Do you see this thick branch? Go fetch!"

Mitch pitched the branch.

"Catch!" said Mitch.

"Fetch the branch, Chip!"

4

Did Chip catch

that branch?

Did Chip fetch

that branch?

Chip just sat on the
bench. He had an itch
on his chin.

"Do you have an itch?"
said Mitch. "Let's get
you a bath."

Chip jumped over the
bench and a ditch, and
ran down a path. Mitch
didn't catch him!